M·O·V·I·E

MUSICALS

M·O·V·I·E
MUSICALS

by Andréa Staskowski

Lerner Publications Company
Minneapolis

Acknowledgments

The photographs in this book are reproduced through the courtesy of: pp. 1, 6, 9, Museum of Modern Art/Film Stills Archive; pp. 2, 10, 24, 40, 45 (bottom), 48, 49, 53, 57, 58, 61, 62, 75, Photofest; pp. 14, 17, 21, 38, 39, 45 (top), 52, Cleveland Public Library; pp. 18, 22, 28, 30, 32, 37, 42, 50, 64, 67, 69, 70, 71, 74, Hollywood Book and Poster.

Front and back cover photographs courtesy of Photofest.

LIBRARY OF CONGRESS CATALOGING-IN-PUBLICATION DATA

Staskowski, Andréa.
   Movie musicals / by Andréa Staskowski.
     p.   cm.
   Includes bibliographical references and index.
   Summary: Discusses the musical film genre and gives analysis and plot summaries of several notable musicals, including "Top Hat," "Meet Me in St. Louis," "Singin' in the Rain," "West Side Story," "Grease," and "Dirty Dancing."
   ISBN 0-8225-1639-X
   1. Musical films—History and criticism—Juvenile literature.
[1. Musical films—History and criticism.] I. Title.
PN1995.9.M86S74   1992
791.43′6—dc20   92-13421
                                CIP
                                AC

Manufactured in the United States of America

1 2 3 4 5 6 97 96 95 94 93 92

Contents

Vaudeville star Al Jolson played the lead in *The Jazz Singer*, the first
sound movie—and the first musical.

Introduction

The movie musical made its first appearance with the invention of sound movies, or the "talkies." The first talking picture, Warner Bros.' *The Jazz Singer,* released in 1927, was also the first movie musical. Even before then, movies and music were linked. Silent movies were accompanied by live musical performances, ranging from a single piano player to a full orchestra. Before theaters devoted exclusively to movies opened for business, movies were often sandwiched between musicians and magicians in the variety shows of the vaudeville stage. *The Jazz Singer* featured the well-known vaudeville performer Al Jolson.

The musical quickly became one of the best-loved film genres in the United States. A musical can be defined simply as a film in which songs and dances play an important part. The standard forms of the movie musical — the "backstage" musical and the "integrated" musical — were firmly established by the early 1930s. The musical flourished in the 1930s and 1940s, considered the golden age of the genre, when Hollywood studios, especially MGM and Warner Bros., released dozens of movie musicals.

In the backstage musical, the musical production numbers are part of a show that is being staged within the film. The king of the backstage musical was a choreographer/director named Busby Berkeley. He directed the musical numbers for such well-known films as *Gold Diggers of 1933, Gold Diggers of 1935, 42nd Street* (1933), *Dames* (1934), and *For Me and My Gal* (1942). These movies were about "putting on the show"—shows that featured extravagant stagings of complicated dance movements. Berkeley became famous for his unusual and creative camera movements, such as filming a dance number from straight overhead.

In the integrated musical, the musical numbers develop as part of the story—there's no show being staged within the movie. Fred Astaire and Ginger Rogers, in films such as *Top Hat,* released in 1935, bring together music and romance, dancing gracefully into courtship. Their singing and dancing emerge "naturally" as an expression of their emotions. Many of the characters Astaire played were professional dancers, which gave him more opportunities to perform within the storyline of the movie.

A couple's romance forms the central concern of many movie musicals. When the couple dances their final joyful dance, the audience knows that the pair will live happily ever after and that all is well in the world.

Another type of musical, the folk musical, stresses the importance of community more than the romance of a particular couple. For instance, in *Meet Me in St. Louis* (1944), directed by Vincente Minnelli, singing and dancing are motivated as much by a love of ordinary life and the celebration of family as by romance. The romantic couple is

Above: Busby Berkeley directs a scene from *42nd Street*. **Below:** The big production numbers in *42nd Street* called for many dancers.

Gene Kelly and Debbie Reynolds kick up their heels in *Singin' in the Rain.*

still important in the folk musical, but it's the woman who is the main focus. Her role is to bring her romantic partner into the community and make sure that the community continues to thrive and the family is held together.

Another important aspect of musicals is that they often treat entertainment itself as subject matter. Usually when we watch a movie, we tend to forget that it isn't real—that the movie was made for our entertainment. For example, when we watch a science fiction movie, we know that a flying saucer didn't really land on earth, but part of the fun is pretending that it did happen. Some musicals, however, such as *Singin' in the Rain* (1952), directed by Stanley Donen and Gene Kelly, show the process of how movies are made. As members of the film audience, we have the impression that we are part of the on-screen audience as well.

West Side Story, a 1961 Robert Wise and Jerome Robbins collaboration, uses contemporary music to celebrate both romantic love and the importance of family in a community threatened by gang warfare. This folk musical shows that the romantic couple's success depends on the support of family and community.

During the 1970s, many Americans lost confidence in traditional community values. U.S. troops withdrew from the war in Vietnam without achieving the goals they had set out to meet. The Watergate scandal made people suspicious of government. In response to this anxiety, Americans longed for simpler times when the United States was the undisputed world leader and most people agreed on what was right and wrong.

With no easy solutions to these problems in sight, Americans looked to the past. During the 1970s, people became nostalgic for the 1950s. *Grease,* about a high school romance in the 1950s, first appeared as a stage play on Broadway in 1972, but it came to the screen at the height of the nostalgia craze, in 1978. The rock and roll sound track, the energetic dancing, and the happily-ever-after ending all made *Grease* very popular.

Dirty Dancing (1987), directed by Emile Ardolino, involves the preparation for two stage shows and tells the story of a young woman's coming of age. The film is something of a mix of the backstage and integrated musical forms, and of the romantic couple musical and the folk musical. After intensive rehearsals for their dance performance, the young woman and her partner begin to fall in love when they dance together in private. But the film does not end there. Later the couple dance together in front of everyone. They are joined by family, friends, and resort staff and guests. Everyone dances together, affirming the community's ideal of a society in which all people are equal.

The musical has changed considerably since its beginnings. The "classical" musical stars—Fred Astaire, Ginger Rogers, Gene Kelly, and Judy Garland—were talented singers and dancers. The movies they starred in showcased both song and dance. More recent musicals have tended to focus on one or the other—either song or dance. For example, in *Dirty Dancing,* no character even pretends to sing. And then there are films such as *Flashdance,* a dance movie in which the leading actress doesn't perform most of the dances—a stand-in does!

Despite the changes, the musical is in no danger of dying. The power of song and dance to stir our emotions and lift our spirits ensures that moviemakers will continue to make musical magic.

Note: The following abbreviations are used in this book:
b/w black and white
dir director
pro producer
sc screenplay by
st starring

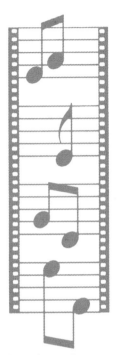

(1935)

TOP HAT

b/w
dir Mark Sandrich
pro Pandro S. Berman
sc Dwight Taylor and Allan Scott, adapted from a play
by Alexander Farago and Laszlo Aladar
music and lyrics Irving Berlin
choreography Fred Astaire with Hermes Pan
st Fred Astaire (Jerry Travers), Ginger Rogers (Dale
Tremont), Edward Everett Horton (Horace
Hardwick), Erik Rhodes (Alberto Beddini), Eric
Blore (Bates)

As dance partners, Fred Astaire and Ginger Rogers, or "Fred and Ginger," created an ideal of romance and grace that is unmatched in the history of film. In their first movie together, *Flying Down to Rio* (1933), Astaire and Rogers did not play the leading roles. But they created such a sensation when they danced that producers hurried to find bigger roles for the couple. Their later movies include *The Gay Divorcee* (1934), *Swing Time* (1936), and *Shall We Dance* (1937).

Top Hat, their fourth of nine films together, was the first one designed especially to showcase their singing and dancing talents. The famous composer Irving Berlin was hired to write the score. Dwight Taylor's job was to build a story around Berlin's songs. His script includes roles for actors

13

Edward Everett Horton, Eric Blore, and Erik Rhodes, regulars in Astaire-Rogers films. Plot devices familiar from their other movies, such as mistaken identity, were also used. But plot wasn't what made the movie great—the dancing was.

For *Top Hat's* famous "Cheek to Cheek" number, Rogers wears her most memorable gown, made of blue silk and ostrich feathers. Though beautiful, the dress caused problems during the filming—feathers flew everywhere. After that Astaire's nickname for Rogers was "Feathers."

"I'm in Heaven"

A cough breaks the rule of silence in the Thackeray Club of London, and the entire roomful of tuxedo-clad men turn to stare at Jerry Travers, the star of Horace Hardwick's new musical revue. When Horace finally arrives to rescue Jerry from the stuffy reading room, Jerry exits with a flourish of tap steps.

In Jerry's hotel room, Horace tells him that after the opening-night performance, they will fly to Italy, where Horace's wife, Madge, has arranged for Jerry to meet one of her young friends. "Is this a weekend or a wedding?" Jerry asks. He begins singing "No Strings": "No ties to my affections/I'm fancy free and free for anything fancy," and then starts to dance.

On the floor below, Dale Tremont is trying to sleep. She calls the manager, who calls Horace. Horace goes downstairs to speak with Dale. Meanwhile she comes upstairs to find Jerry dancing with a statuette. Dale complains to Jerry about the noise, but as she walks toward the elevator, she smiles. Jerry scatters sand from an ashtray onto the floor and does a quiet shuffle to lull Dale to sleep on the floor below.

The next morning, Jerry surprises Dale by driving her horse-drawn cab to the stables. She goes horseback riding by herself until a sudden downpour forces her to take shelter in a small pavilion. Jerry pulls up with the horse and carriage, offering to rescue her. Dale acts aloof until the thunder sends her scurrying toward him. Jerry begins to sing "Isn't This a Lovely Day (to be caught in the rain)": "The weather is frightening/The thunder and lightening seem to be having their way/As far as I'm concerned it's a lovely day." When he steps onto the floor and whistles, she whistles the tune in reply. Then she joins him in dance, matching his every step.

Later, smiling and humming, Dale enters her hotel room to find it full of flowers sent by Jerry. She tells her business partner, the clothing designer Alberto Beddini, that she wants to stay in London because she is in love. But she doesn't know the man's name! Beddini would prefer that she follow their original plan—to visit Madge Hardwick in Italy so that Dale can show off his clothing collection to Madge's rich friends. A telegram from Madge arrives saying that her husband, Horace, is staying at Dale's hotel. Madge suggests that Dale look him up.

That evening, Dale asks the hotel manager to identify Mr. Hardwick. He points to a man with a briefcase and cane on the balcony. With a chandelier blocking her view, Dale can't see Horace handing his briefcase and cane to Jerry. When Jerry comes downstairs with the briefcase and cane, Dale thinks he is Madge's husband, Horace Hardwick. As Jerry approaches Dale, she greets him with a slap.

Distressed, Dale wonders why Madge's husband flirted with her. Beddini convinces Dale to go to Italy to tell Madge about her husband's behavior. Meanwhile the hotel management is investigating the cause of the slap. Horace, terrified

Horace worries that Jerry's landed himself in trouble.

that Jerry will be involved in a scandal that will ruin the big show, sends his butler, Bates, to follow Dale.

At the theater before the opening, Horace reads a telegram from Madge suggesting that he meet her friend Dale Tremont. Just then Jerry realizes that the woman he is in love with is Dale. He insists that Horace charter a plane so they can fly to Italy as soon as the show is over. Onstage Jerry performs "Top Hat, White Tie, and Tails," in front of a chorus of male dancers.

Poolside in Italy, Madge asks Dale if Horace looked her up. When Dale says that she found Horace fascinating, Madge asks if Horace flirted with her. To Dale's reply that Horace sent her a roomful of flowers, Madge simply shrugs and says, "When you're as old as I am, you take your men as you find them—if you can find them." Dale is shocked.

Then Madge explains the real reason she invited Dale to Italy—to introduce her to a prospective husband. "Despite the fact that all men are male," says Madge, "there is nothing so secure as a good reliable husband."

As soon as Horace and Jerry arrive in Italy, Madge asks Horace about Dale. He denies that he's met her. Upon hearing from Madge that "Horace" forgot her, Dale decides to teach him a lesson. She goes up to Jerry's hotel room and puts her arms around him, talking about their romance in Paris. Since Jerry hasn't been in Paris since he was ten years old, he knows this is some kind of gag and he exaggerates her story even further. Dale is exasperated.

That evening at dinner, Madge encourages Dale to dance with Jerry because Jerry is the man she has selected as a husband for Dale. Dale still thinks Jerry is Horace and thus married to Madge. Madge urges them to dance closer. Finally Dale says, "Well, if Madge doesn't care, I certainly don't," and she relaxes into Jerry's arms as he sings "Cheek to Cheek": "Heaven, I'm in heaven/and my heart beats so that I can hardly speak/and I seem to find the happiness I seek/when we're out together dancing cheek to cheek." They dance together across the floor and onto a balcony, he in white tie and tails, she in a satin and feather gown.

At the end of their passionate dance, Dale again looks uneasy. She does, after all, think he is married. So when Jerry says in all sincerity, "Marry me!" she slaps him in the face.

Alberto Beddini tries to console Dale. "Why don't you marry me?" he offers. "I'm rich, I'm pretty." Dale agrees, as long as they do it quickly.

When Madge receives the news that Dale has married Beddini, Madge turns to Horace and says it's all his fault. With that, Jerry realizes that Dale has mistaken him for

Horace. He rushes to the room above the bridal suite where Dale and Beddini are staying. He interrupts their embrace by dancing. Jerry convinces Dale to go for a ride in a gondola so he can explain everything.

Beddini, Horace, and Madge take off in a boat to find Jerry and Dale. Meanwhile, Jerry and Dale return to shore as the group's boat runs out of gas. This gives Jerry and Dale time alone to enjoy the wedding supper, complete with a cake topped by a bride and groom that had been prepared for Dale and Beddini. An ensemble of dancers performs "The Piccolino." Dale sings the song, explaining the new dance number to Jerry. And then they dance.

The would-be rescuers return. Madge warns Dale that Beddini is furious. Jerry tells Beddini that he wants to marry Dale. Just then Horace and Bates, the butler, rush in. Bates explains that he used a number of different disguises while he was following Dale, including that of a clergyman. Bates "married" Dale and Beddini—so they're not really married at all. Hand in hand, Jerry and Dale go off dancing.

AN IDEAL MATCH

One explanation commonly given for Fred and Ginger's success is that "he gave her class and she gave him sex appeal." There is at least a hint of truth in this. Before he teamed up with Ginger, Fred danced with his sister Adele. When Adele Astaire retired in 1932, some people in Hollywood were concerned about whether Fred would make it as a star in his own right. He had never appeared in a show without Adele as a dance partner, and she was generally regarded as more appealing romantically than the slightly balding Fred.

Ginger Rogers changed all that. She was younger than Fred, 22 to his 34 when they made their first film together.

Ginger and Fred—a match made in heaven

And when the youthful and lively Rogers gazed at Astaire, her look of desire was utterly convincing. Her previous film roles as working girls helped make it believable that Astaire would offer her a more refined life. As a couple, Fred and Ginger overcame their own limitations. They made an ideal match.

MEET ME IN ST. LOUIS

color
dir Vincente Minnelli
pro Arthur Freed
sc Irving Brecher and Fred F. Finklehoffer from stories
    by Sally Benson
music director George Stoll
music numbers Ralph Blane and Hugh Martin
choreography Charles Walters
st Judy Garland (Esther Smith), Margaret O'Brien
    (Tootie Smith), Lucille Bremer (Rose Smith), Mary
    Astor (Mrs. Anna Smith), Leon Ames (Mr. Alonzo
    Smith), Tom Drake (John Truett)

When the MGM studio bought the rights to Sally Benson's nostalgic stories about her childhood in the Midwest, the scriptwriters suggested heightening the drama by adding a kidnapping. According to director Vincente Minnelli, the studio said, "There's no story here. A man wants to take his family to New York and they don't want to go. That's no story." Producer Arthur Freed was only able to make this film about the joys and disappointments of family life—with no kidnapping—because *Oklahoma!,* which also celebrated life in the Midwest, was a big success on Broadway that year.

Vincente Minnelli jumped at the chance to direct the film. It is set in a place not unlike his hometown, Chicago, and it takes place in the year of his birth. Minnelli's future wife,

23

Producer Arthur Freed taps out a tune as director Vincente Minnelli listens. Minnelli married Judy Garland in 1945.

Judy Garland, was less enthusiastic about her part. She felt she had already played too many teenage girls and was ready for more mature roles. As it turned out, *Meet Me in St. Louis* was one of Garland's warmest and most memorable performances.

"Right Here in Our Hometown"

A sepia-toned photograph of a Victorian home in St. Louis, Missouri, comes alive. It is the summer of 1903, and the center of the household's activity is the kitchen. Katie, the maid, and Mrs. Anna Smith discuss how much sugar to put in the ketchup. Agnes, age 12, begins to sing "Meet Me in St. Louis" and Grandpa picks up the tune. When 17-year-old Esther comes in, she's also singing the song.

Esther pleads with Katie to serve dinner an hour early because Rose, the Smiths' oldest daughter, is expecting a long-distance telephone call from her boyfriend, Warren, in New York. Esther thinks Warren is calling to propose to Rose, and as far as she's concerned it's about time Rose, who is 20, got married. Meanwhile, Esther has romantic plans of her own. She has decided she is going to marry the young man who just moved in next door, John Truett—even though they have not yet met! Gazing at John from across the yard, Esther sings "The Boy Next Door": "The moment I saw him smile/I knew he was just my style/My only regret is that we've never met/though I dream of him all the while."

As the dinner preparations continue, Mrs. Smith warns the children not to say a word to their father about Rose's phone call. As he walks up the path to the house, Mr. Smith hears Esther and Rose singing "Meet Me in St. Louis." He is hot, exasperated, and sick of that song. When told that dinner will be served early, Mr. Smith says they will find a new maid if Katie can't serve dinner at 6:30 as usual.

When dinner is finally served at 6:30, Katie tries to speed the meal along, but Mr. Smith resists. The phone rings. Mr. Smith answers. He misunderstands the operator and hangs up. Esther explains why Rose is sobbing by telling Mr. Smith that he has ruined the girl's chances for marriage. Realizing that everyone knew about the phone call but him, Mr. Smith becomes very angry. Nevertheless, when the phone rings again, he lets Esther answer. The conversation with Warren is anticlimactic; they talk about the weather. The family relaxes and enjoys the meal.

John Truett has accepted the invitation to the party Rose is giving for her brother Lon before he goes away to college. Though Esther is eager to meet John, she waits until all the guests have arrived before she joins the party downstairs. When Lon introduces John to Esther, she pretends she has never seen him before. Guests play the trumpet, fiddle, and piano, and the entire party joins in singing and dancing "Skip to My Lou." The youngest Smith sister, five-year-old Tootie, sings a sailor's drinking tune by herself. Then Tootie and Esther do the cakewalk to "Under the Bamboo Tree."

All the guests leave, but John Truett can't find his hat. Esther gets it for him, from the bread box, where she has hidden it. She invites him to join the crowd on Friday evening when they go visit the fairgrounds, where the World's Fair will be held next year. John says he would like to go, if basketball practice doesn't run late. Esther then asks if he would be so kind as to help her turn off the lights throughout the house. As each lamp dims, the atmosphere becomes increasingly romantic. He asks her about the words to a song and she sings. They stand face to face. Esther is poised for a kiss. John breaks the romantic mood by vigorously shaking her hand and thanking her for a wonderful evening. He leaves.

The next Friday, Esther looks around nervously as her friends board the streetcar to the fairgrounds. With no sign of John, she boards the trolley. The others on the trolley sing "The Trolley Song." "Clang, clang, clang, went the trolley," they sing while she remains silent. When she sees John running to get on the streetcar, Esther joins in the song. Finally, John makes his way to the seat next to her.

It is now the autumn of 1903. Rose helps her sisters Agnes and Tootie dress up as ghosts for Halloween. Instead of going trick-or-treating, these children go door to door "killing" their neighbors by throwing flour in their faces. As the children divide into groups, Tootie is left out because she is too little. Refusing to be sent home, Tootie volunteers to take on the most "dangerous" neighbor, Mr. Brokoff, by herself. After the man opens the door, Tootie throws the flour in his face, then runs off, terrified.

Rose and Esther are on the front porch when they hear Tootie screaming. Esther runs off and finds Tootie hurt and carries her into the house. The family members hover around Tootie while they wait for the doctor. She tells them that John Truett tried to kill her. No one believes this, but when the doctor pries open Tootie's fist to find a clump of hair, it's clear there was a struggle. Esther rushes next door and starts slugging John Truett.

While Tootie is settling into bed, Agnes comes home. As they begin talking, the truth comes out. John Truett didn't try to kill Tootie—he tried to save her from the police! Tootie and Agnes had put a dummy on the trolley-car tracks and the police were looking for the pranksters. At first Esther is angry, then she laughs with the others and runs next door to apologize to John. John accepts her apology, invites her out for the next evening, and kisses her for the first time.

Mr. Smith returns home while the rest of the family is sitting down to eat ice cream. He has an announcement. He has accepted a position as head of his law firm's New York office. The family greets the news with shock and horror. Mrs. Smith worries that it will be hard for the children to make the adjustment. "It's all settled," Mr. Smith declares. "We're moving to New York." He begins to cut the cake Katie made, but no one wants a piece. Eventually, they all go upstairs, leaving Mr. and Mrs. Smith alone. "I'm treated like I'm a criminal," he says. "I'm trying to provide my family with everything they deserve."

Mrs. Smith sits down at the piano while Mr. Smith eats his cake. Then she begins singing the familiar tune

Rose and Esther sing together at the piano.

"Together." "Through the years, we'll still be together," she sings. The family members gather around the piano, pick up their dessert plates, and enjoy their cake together.

The winter of 1903 has left St. Louis covered in snow. The Smith siblings build snowmen and women and discuss the upcoming Christmas dance. Neither Rose nor Lon have escorts, because Warren, Rose's beau, is bringing a girl named Lucille instead. Esther, who will be going with John Truett, convinces her brother and sister to accompany one another to the dance. They will all be there for their last dance in St. Louis.

While she is dressing for the dance, Esther receives an unexpected visit from John. He explains that he won't be able to take her to the dance because he doesn't have a tuxedo. Esther is terribly disappointed. When Grandpa hears her crying, he offers to escort her to the dance.

Later, to Esther's surprise, John manages to get a tuxedo in time for the last dance. As they say good-night after the dance, John asks Esther to marry him. He can't bear the thought of being parted from her when Esther moves to New York with her family. Esther is overjoyed by his proposal, but she is not yet 18 and John has not finished college. They will have to wait until they are ready for marriage.

Back at home, Esther finds Tootie at her bedroom window waiting for Santa Claus. Esther sings "Have Yourself a Merry Little Christmas" to her. Tootie leaps up and races to the yard, where she smashes the snow people. "Nobody is going to have them if we're not taking them to New York," she cries. Esther tries to comfort her. Mr. Smith observes the scene from Tootie's bedroom window. Afterwards he calls for his wife and the rest of the family. "We're not moving to New York," he announces. "We're going to stay here until we rot." In the middle of Mr. Smith's speech, Warren bursts into the house. "I've positively decided," he shouts, pointing at Rose, "that we're going to get married at the earliest possible opportunity. That's final. I love you." Then he walks out. The Smith family gather around the tree and open their Christmas presents.

In the spring of 1904, all the Smith girls are dressed in white, wearing hats and carrying parasols. Warren and John pick up Rose and Esther. The rest of the family piles into a second carriage as they all go off to the World's Fair, where they meet Lon and Lucille. They marvel at the magnificence of the fair. "There's never been anything like it in the whole world," says Mrs. Smith. "It's right here in our hometown," adds Rose. "It's right here where we live," says Esther, "right here in St. Louis."

John, Tootie, and Esther enjoy a soda.

WARTIME ANXIETIES

Meet Me in St. Louis colorfully celebrates the family and life in the heartland of America. Nevertheless, there's a dark side to the film. Mr. Smith, the head of the family, is frequently treated as if he were completely unnecessary— except that he provides the family's income. Second, the threat that the family will have to move to a large, distant city creates tension.

These anxieties can be traced to World War II, which was going on when the movie was made. Soldiers were drafted "for the duration" of the war. By 1944 many men had already been away from home for more than two years, with no return date in sight. Women were running households on their own. Men felt as though they were not part of the family and were no longer needed. Furthermore, changing economic conditions forced many people to leave small towns during the 1940s to find work in big cities. The movie expressed some people's fears and then put those fears to rest.

SINGIN' IN THE RAIN

color
pro Arthur Freed
dir Gene Kelly and Stanley Donen
sc Betty Comden and Adolph Green from the play by
   Betty Comden and Adolph Green
music director Lennie Hayton
songs Arthur Freed, Nacio Herb Brown, Betty
   Comden, and Roger Eden
st Gene Kelly (Don Lockwood), Donald O'Connor
   (Cosmo Brown), Debbie Reynolds (Kathy Selden),
   Jean Hagen (Lina Lamont), Millard Mitchell (R. F.
   Simpson), Cyd Charisse (Dancer)

While he was praised most for his lively, spontaneous dancing style, Gene Kelly had many other talents as well. Even before he received a special Academy Award in 1951, "in appreciation of his versatility as an actor, singer, director, and dancer, and especially for his brilliant achievements in the art of choreography on film," Gene Kelly had already demonstrated a variety of skills in his jobs as dance instructor, gas station attendant, and ditch digger.

When producer Arthur Freed gave Kelly the opportunity to direct a movie, the then 37-year-old Kelly chose Stanley Donen as his codirector. Donen had already worked with Kelly as a choreographer, but everyone was nervous that the 24-year-old former dancer wouldn't be up to the task of directing. There was no reason to worry. The three pictures Donen and Kelly codirected are among Hollywood's most inventive musicals—*On the Town* (1949), *Singin' in the Rain,* and *It's Always Fair Weather* (1955). All three movies share a natural, fluid sense of movement and an energy rooted in everyday life.

"Gotta Dance"

A crowd has assembled for the premiere of Hollywood's latest silent film, *Royal Rascals.* Finally the film's stars arrive—"the romantic lovers of the screen who are a household word all over the world"—Don Lockwood and Lina Lamont. As the two step out of their limousine, the fans go wild. Asked to tell the story of his success, Don begins by acknowledging his lifelong friend, Cosmo Brown. Then Don tells his adoring fans, "There is one motto I always live by. Dignity. Always dignity."

He goes on to say he had a privileged and refined upbringing, but we see him as a boy dancing with Cosmo in a pool hall and getting kicked out. The rest of his life story proceeds similarly—then he breaks into the movies as a stunt man on one of Lina's pictures. She ignores him until R. F. Simpson, the head of the studio, announces that Don will star opposite Lina in her next picture. Then it's Don's turn to ignore her. Now they are a screen sensation with another smash hit.

After the film is shown, Don thanks the enthusiastic crowd. Backstage, Lina screeches in a high-pitched voice, "What's the big idea? Can't a girl get a word in edgewise?" R. F., Cosmo, Don, and the head of the publicity department exchange knowing looks. "It's better if Don does all the talking," they tell her. "What's wrong with the way I talk?" she shouts. The publicity man sends Lina off to the premiere party with R. F.; Don rides with Cosmo. Don is exasperated with Lina. She thinks they are engaged because that's what the fan magazines say.

On the way to the party, Cosmo's expensive car gets a flat tire. Don's fans spot him and mob him. He escapes by jumping into a convertible driven by a young woman. "You're a criminal," she screams, "I recognize your face." She hails a policeman, who immediately recognizes Don Lockwood. Once she finds out who he is, the woman offers to drive Don to Beverly Hills. Kathy Selden is shocked at how the fans treated Don. He tries to take advantage of her sympathy, putting his arm around her. Realizing what he's up to, Kathy acts uninterested in Don's career and goes so far as to say that screen acting isn't acting at all. Don is taken aback.

At the party, R. F. announces a surprise—a talking picture screen test. The crowd watches it with disbelief. But R. F. tells them that "Warner Bros. is making a whole talking picture, *The Jazz Singer.*"

The floor show then begins and who pops out of a cake but Kathy Selden! After the chorus finishes its number, Don asks Kathy if he can drive her home. She responds by aiming a cream pie at Don. Lina steps in the way and gets the pie in her face. Don runs after Kathy, but she's already driven off.

At the studio the next day, Don meets up with Cosmo. Hearing the story of Don's next film, *The Duelling Cavaliers,* Cosmo jokes, "Seen one, you've seen them all." "That's what Kathy Selden said," moans Don. To ease his friend's worries, Cosmo performs a comic dance number, "Make 'Em Laugh."

On the set of *The Duelling Cavaliers,* Lina tells Don that she got Kathy fired from her job. As they go through the motions of their love scene, Don calls Lina a snake. R. F.

interrupts the shooting. "Tell everyone to go home," he says. *The Jazz Singer* is a huge success and the public only wants talking pictures; *The Duelling Cavaliers* will have to be a talking picture. Lina speaks up just then—and Don and R. F. know they have a problem.

Kathy Selden is a member of the chorus for the musical numbers in the sound pictures the studio is now producing. R. F. sees that she has talent and selects her for a larger role in an upcoming picture. Cosmo brings Don onto the set to see Kathy.

Kathy and Don walk through the studio lot. She asks about his romance with Lina, which she's read about in the fan magazines. She admits to having seen all of Don's movies and to being a fan herself. Don wants to be romantic but needs the proper setting. They enter an empty stage, where, through the magic of movie technology, he creates a sunset, mist, lights in a garden, a balcony, stardust, and a soft summer breeze. He sings to her, "You Were Meant for Me": "You were meant for me/I was meant for you." They dance together.

Diction coaches, who teach the silent stars how to speak for the talkies, have never been busier. Lina isn't doing very well with her lessons, however; she continues to shriek. Don is doing quite well when Cosmo interrupts his lesson. He begins making faces and soon he and Don turn the lesson into a hilarious song and dance number, "Moses (supposes his toeses are roses)."

Don, Kathy, and Cosmo arrive together for the sneak preview of *The Duelling Cavaliers,* but Don and Kathy have to sit separately so as not to upset Lina. As soon as the picture begins, it is apparent that it is a disaster. The best part of the movie is when the sound goes out of sync. The audience howls with laughter.

"Good morning, good morning to you," harmonize Cosmo, Kathy, and Don.

That evening, Don, Kathy, and Cosmo have a snack in Don's mansion. "Lockwood and Lamont are through," he says. "They're museum pieces." Cosmo comes up with the idea to turn *The Duelling Cavaliers* into a musical. As they excitedly discuss the project, they realize they've been talking all night and sing "Good Morning." They come up with a solution to the problem of Lina's inability to sing or speak on-screen. Kathy will lip-sync Lina's lines.

Don sees Kathy home, then sends his car away. Even though it is raining, Don is so in love with Kathy he feels as if the sun were shining. He strolls down the street and sings "Singin' in the Rain" while splashing in puddles.

The next day, R. F. agrees to make *The Duelling Cavaliers* into a musical, now to be called *The Dancing Cavaliers*. Kathy and Don sing the love songs together in the recording studio while Lina simply pretends to sing the words on the set. The last thing left to do is the modern number, "Gotta Dance/Broadway Melody," the story of a young dancer who comes to New York to become a star. At a nightclub, Don dances with the sultry girlfriend of a gangster. Later he sings "Gotta Dance" and the entire company joins him in the finale.

The lively "Gotta Dance" number

Don is excited to work with Kathy.

Afterwards, with Don, Kathy rerecords Lina's dialogue. Don declares his love for Kathy and vows to tell the whole world. Lina enters. She has found out that Kathy will get screen credit for doing Lina's singing and dancing. When Lina hears that a publicity campaign has been planned for Kathy, Lina storms out.

The next day, the newspapers are filled with stories about Lina's great musical abilities. She has gone to the papers herself before the publicity department could get there. According to Lina's contract, she controls her publicity, and if the studio says anything negative about her, she can sue. Trapped, R. F. removes Kathy's screen credit.

Singin' in the Rain is Hollywood magic at its best.

The night of the premiere, the picture is a hit. Backstage, Lina announces that Kathy is going to go right on singing for her. When Don, Cosmo, and R. F. protest that Kathy has a career of her own, Lina responds, "Listen to that applause. You're not going to give away that gold mine." Lina says she is going onstage to thank the fans. This time, no one stops her. She speaks in her usual high-pitched nasal voice and with bad grammar. The audience is stunned. Don and R. F. insist that Kathy sing for Lina from behind the curtain. She begins, "Singin' in the Rain." Without warning, Don, Cosmo, and R. F. pull open the curtain to reveal Kathy singing. Then Cosmo jumps in to sing for Kathy, making it obvious that Lina isn't the real singer. Lina runs off the stage, Kathy runs down the aisle, and Don runs onstage calling after Kathy. "That's the girl whose voice you heard and loved tonight," he tells the audience. "She's the real star of the picture, Kathy Selden." He sings to her, "You Are My Lucky Star." Kathy joins in.

Later, we see Don's face on a billboard—an advertisement for *Singin' in the Rain,* the new Don Lockwood and Kathy Selden picture. We hear them singing and then see them kiss in front of the billboard. They are together in "real life" as well as in the movies.

REALITY OR FANTASY?

The last scene in *Singin' in the Rain* is a good example of how the movies, especially musicals, try to blur the distinction between reality and fantasy. Throughout the film, we see how movies and the media create a false reality. Lina Lamont thinks that she and Don Lockwood are in love because they are the "romantic lovers of the screen." She believes this even when Don tells her there is nothing between them. Kathy Selden also thinks that the love scenes

Don and Kathy are supposed to be a couple in "real life" as well as in the movies. But Gene Kelly and Debbie Reynolds, the actors, did not have a real-life romance.

between Lina and Don are too convincing to be faked. And the fan magazines say they are engaged.

Don tells her not to believe all that nonsense. But when he wants to declare his love for Kathy, he uses movie technology to create a romantic setting. After showing how Hollywood's "dream machine" isn't real, *Singin' in the Rain* starts the whole process up again. On the one hand, the movie tells us that its vision of love and happiness isn't true, or real. On the other hand, it asks us to believe that everything we watch on the screen is real. In the movies' version of reality, good wins and true love overcomes all obstacles.

(1961)

WEST SIDE STORY

color
pro Robert Wise
dir Robert Wise and Jerome Robbins
sc Ernest Lehman based on a book by Arthur Laurents
music direction Saul Chaplin
music and lyrics Leonard Bernstein and Stephen Sondheim
choreography Jerome Robbins
st Natalie Wood (Maria), Richard Beymer (Tony), Russ Tamblyn (Riff), Rita Moreno (Anita), George Chakiris (Bernardo)

West Side Story opened as a Broadway musical on September 26, 1957. Its subject matter—gang warfare—was up-to-date while its reworking of Shakespeare's *Romeo and Juliet* gave it universal appeal. At the time, Hollywood was keen on making theatrical musicals into movies. The director and choreographer of the stage production, Jerome Robbins, was hired to work with film director Robert Wise to adapt the play to the screen. It was not a happy pairing. Robbins and Wise had so many disagreements that Robbins quit before the last two musical numbers were choreographed. Nonetheless, Robbins and Wise share the director's credit and an Academy Award for Best Director. Robbins also received a special award from the academy for his choreography.

The female lead did not, however, dance in the film. Because she had no formal dance training, Natalie Wood was given just a few simple steps to perform while the camera moved around her to create the illusion of dancing. Furthermore, neither Wood nor her costar, Richard Beymer, did their own singing! Wood's songs were performed by Marni Dixon, who would later be Audrey Hepburn's "voice" in *My Fair Lady*. Jimmy Bryant's voice was dubbed in for Beymer's songs.

John Astin didn't sing or dance in *West Side Story*, but his film debut as the recreation director marked the beginning of a highly successful acting career. He played Gomez Addams on "The Addams Family" television program.

"There's a Place for Us"

In a concrete courtyard in Manhattan, a group of blond teenage boys disrupt a basketball game, then move on. As they cross the street, the members of this gang, the Jets, slide into jazz dance steps. The Jets confront a dark-haired boy who is part of a rival gang, the Sharks. Finally, the two gangs, formed along racial lines — whites versus Puerto Ricans — face each other and declare war.

The Jets prepare for a "rumble," which will determine which gang will control Manhattan's West Side. Riff, the leader of the Jets, wants Tony to assist him in the fight as his lieutenant. But Tony now has a job working for Doc, the kindly old owner of a candy store, and he wants no part of the fight. Instead he tells Riff about his dream of reaching for something. He sings "Something's Coming": "Something's coming, something good, maybe tonight." But Riff's reply, the "Jet Song," convinces Tony to come to the dance, where the gangs will meet.

Meanwhile, Maria and Anita get ready for the dance.

Members of the Jets confront one of the Sharks, then dance to the energetic "Jet Song."

Maria and Anita are the sister and fiancée of Bernardo, the leader of the Sharks. "Tonight," says Maria, who recently arrived from Puerto Rico, "is the real beginning of my life as a young lady in America."

At the dance, the Jets and the Sharks stake out opposite sides of the room. To ease the tension, the recreation coordinator suggests a "get together" dance. Reluctantly both gangs participate, and the dance turns into a mambo competition, "Dance at the Gym." Amid the energetic performances, Maria's and Tony's eyes meet. They approach one another and do a few simple dance steps together. Tony, overwhelmed by the intensity of the encounter, asks Maria, "Are you joking with me?" "I haven't learned to joke like that," replies Maria, "and now I never will."

Bernardo is infuriated when he sees Maria and Tony dancing. He insists that Maria leave immediately. Riff and Bernardo set up a war council meeting for midnight at Doc's store. Tony wanders off, repeating Maria's name. He sings "Maria": "Maria, I just met a girl named Maria."

On the roof, the Sharks and their girlfriends discuss life in America. The girls like America because of the freedom. The boys are angered by racial discrimination and their lack of job and educational opportunities. They sing "America."

Tony walks through the alleys behind the high-rise apartments calling, "Maria." She meets him on the fire escape. "I'm not one of them," he tells her. "You're not one of us," she replies. Tony wants to stay in the magic of the moment. He sings, "Tonight, tonight/It all began tonight/I saw you and the world went away." As they say good-night, he tries to bridge the gap between their worlds. "Buenas noches," he says in parting.

While the Jets wait for the midnight meeting, they hang

out in the street making jokes about their problems at home. In "Gee, Officer Krupke," they sing their way through a series of imaginary conversations with the police, a social worker, a psychiatrist, and others who treat them as juvenile delinquents. They laugh about the stereotype of gang members as "sociologically sick."

At Doc's store, the Jets challenge the Sharks to a rumble that will divide the territory once and for all. They set the time for the next day and discuss weapons. Just then, a police officer enters. To avoid problems with the police, the Jets and Sharks pretend to be friends. The officer begins harassing the Sharks. The Jets stop Bernardo as he moves toward him. The policeman tells the Sharks to "clear out" and pushes the chair out from beneath Bernardo. The Sharks file out of the candy store whistling "My Country 'Tis of Thee." As soon as the Sharks leave, the officer asks where the rumble is going to be. When the Jets refuse to cooperate, he calls them "tinhorn immigrant scum."

The next day, Maria sings and dances through the back room of the bridal shop where she and Anita and several other Puerto Rican girls work. "I feel pretty," she sings, "... because I'm in love with a pretty wonderful boy." At closing time, Maria helps Anita lock up the shop and Anita lets it slip that there's going to be a rumble that night. Just then, Tony walks in. Anita sees how Maria and Tony feel about one another. She is worried.

When Anita leaves, Maria tells Tony that he must stop the fight. Tony agrees and says he will come to her house afterwards to meet her parents. They joke about their mothers' reactions to their romance. They pretend to get married, exchanging vows and "rings."

On the street the mood is quite different. Both sides sing the "Rumble" number: "We're the ones to stop them once

Maria and Tony meet on the fire escape.

The Puerto Rican girls sing "America."

and for all." The Jets and the Sharks prepare for a major battle by arming themselves with belts, rocks, and knives.

The gangs meet under the highway as planned. The rumble begins, heating into a knife fight between Riff and Bernardo. Bernardo stabs Riff. As he falls, Riff hands Tony the knife. In shock, Tony lunges towards Bernardo and kills him. At the sound of police sirens, both gangs split.

Tony screams after stabbing Bernardo.

On the rooftop, Maria dances by herself, anticipating dancing with Tony. Shark member Chino comes up, and Maria asks about Tony. Chino screams, "He killed your brother." Maria cannot believe it. In her room, she prays that it is not true. Tony enters through the window. He explains that it's true he killed Bernardo, but that he didn't mean to do it. "It's not us that's the problem," he tells her, "it's everything around us." They sing "Somewhere": "There's a place for us, somewhere/peace and quiet and open air."

The Jets congregate to decide what to do. To get past the police, the new leader advises they play it cool. Snapping their fingers, the young men dance as they sing "Cool" together. As the Jets take to the streets, a girl tells them about Tony and Maria and says that Chino has a gun and is looking for Tony. He's going to kill him. The Jets spread out to find Tony and warn him.

Tony is with Maria. Anita sees them and cautions Maria in the song "A Boy Like That": "A boy like that will kill your brother/Stick to your own kind." Maria convinces Anita that she loves Tony. The girls sing "I Have a Love" together: "When love comes so strong, there is no right or wrong/ Your love is your life."

The police officer comes to the apartment to question Maria. Maria secretly asks Anita to go to Doc's store to tell Tony she has been detained. Reluctantly, Anita goes. The officer asks who she danced with that upset Bernardo. She tells him it was a Puerto Rican boy.

At Doc's store, Anita tells the Jets that she wants to speak with Doc. They are uncooperative, blowing smoke in her face and saying mean and ugly things about her dark skin and Spanish heritage. Then they start pulling at her clothes, grabbing at her, and throwing her around the room. They are about to rape her when Doc comes in. As Anita gets up, she gives them a message for Tony. "Maria never was going to meet him," she says. "Chino found out and shot her." After Anita leaves, Doc turns to the Jets. "You make this world lousy," he says in disgust. "We didn't make it," says one boy in reply.

Doc goes down to the basement. Tony is brimming with enthusiasm about the life he and Maria are going to have in the country. Doc shakes his head and asks, "Why do you live like there's a war on? Why do you kill?" Maria understands, says Tony. Doc tells him she's dead. In despair, Tony runs through the streets shouting, "Chino, come and get me too. Kill me too." He runs into the playground and sees Maria through the fence. They run toward one another and embrace. A shot rings out. Tony is fatally wounded. Maria holds him in her arms. They sing "Somewhere": "There's a place for us/hold my hand and we're halfway there/hold my hand and I'll take you there/ somehow, someday. . . ." Tony dies.

Maria loses both Bernardo (above) and Tony.

Jerome Robbins and Robert Wise scope out an overhead shot during the filming of *West Side Story.*

The Jets move toward Tony's body. Picking up the gun, Maria points to the Jets and the Sharks. "You all killed him, my brother and Riff," she says. "You all killed him with hate." She drops to the ground and lets go of the gun. The police arrive. Maria rushes to protect Tony from the police. "Don't you touch him," she screams. Finally the Jets come forward to carry Tony's body away. Then, putting aside their differences, the Sharks step in to help. As they all file out, Chino is led away by the police, and Maria stands alone.

TWO DIFFERENT COMMUNITIES

West Side Story shares many characteristics of the traditional folk musical. Although the settings are very different, in both *Meet Me in St. Louis* and *West Side Story,* women are the center of the community. For example, Maria is the one who brings the two warring gangs together, even though she faces tragedy.

In both of these folk musicals, the songs and dances emerge spontaneously. Song and dance, costumes, and setting all contribute to the image of the particular community each film represents. In the streets and tenements of New York's Upper West Side, the white and Puerto Rican gang members cruise the streets with finger-snapping jazz moves. They wear tight jeans and slicked-back hair. The New York of *West Side Story* is a tough environment, and the short, tense musical numbers the gang members sing reflect that tension.

The community of St. Louis in *Meet Me in St. Louis,* on the other hand, is very warm and friendly. The traditional "Skip to My Lou" song and dance number at Lon's going-away party reflects the film's old-fashioned values.

(1978)

GREASE

color
pro Robert Stigwood and Allan Carr
dir Randal Kleiser
sc Bronte Woodward, based on Allan Carr's adaptation
  of the Broadway musical by Jim Jacobs and
  Warren Casey
music and lyrics Barry Gibb
choreography Patricia Birch
st John Travolta (Danny), Olivia Newton-John (Sandy),
  Stockard Channing (Rizzo), Jeff Conaway
  (Kenickie), Eve Arden (Principal), Sid Caesar
  (Coach), Frankie Avalon (Teen Angel)

When producer Allan Carr met Olivia Newton-John at a party, he immediately offered her the role of Sandy in *Grease.* An international pop star with four hit singles and four platinum albums, Newton-John still had stage fright when she performed at concerts. She was so unsure of her ability to act that before she agreed to accept the part in *Grease,* she insisted on seeing a screen test of herself. She needn't have worried. *Grease* went on to make more money than any other musical in history.

"Good-bye to Sandra Dee"

Waves crash onto a secluded, rocky shoreline in southern California as an orchestral version of "Love Is a Many-Splendored Thing" plays. A young couple kiss on the beach. The summer is ending and Sandy's family is returning to Australia. She wonders when she and Danny will be together again. He replies, "It's only the beginning." With that, the film's credits begin. A deejay announces *Grease*, "a new old favorite of mine." Cartoon versions of Sandy and Danny get ready for the first day of school. Then the cartoon image of Rydell High fades into the "real" Rydell, where both Sandy and Danny are seniors but neither knows the other is there.

Danny's leather-jacketed buddies, the T-Birds, want to know all the details about the summer he spent with the girl he met on the beach. Danny struts through the song "Summer Nights." Meanwhile, the pony-tailed Sandy sings her own version of the song to the Pink Ladies, a group of girls friendly with the T-Birds. Sandy skips and licks an ice cream cone as she tells them of her innocent romance. When the tough-talking leader of the Pink Ladies, Rizzo, finds out that Sandy's summer love was Danny, Rizzo smirks.

After a pep rally, the Pink Ladies take Sandy, who is a cheerleader, to the parking lot where the T-Birds hang out. Sandy and Danny are thrilled to see each other. But Danny's friends pressure him to act cool and not show his enthusiasm. Sandy is hurt and confused by his behavior. She runs off crying. Frenchy invites Sandy to her house for a sleep-over with the Pink Ladies.

At Frenchy's, the differences between Sandy and the Pink Ladies become glaringly apparent. Sandy is refined, proper, and sheltered, while the Pink Ladies are, well, less so. Rizzo puts on a blond wig and sings, "Look at Me, I'm Sandra Dee," making fun of Sandy by comparing her to a popular 1950s movie star who had a good-girl image. Then Rizzo climbs out the window to go for a drive with T-Bird leader

Students hang out at Rydell High.

Kenickie. They make out in the back seat of his car.

The next day, Kenickie brings his old car to auto mechanics class to fix it up. The T-Birds joke that it's a piece of junk, except for Danny, who sees the car's potential. He sings "Greased Lightning," joined by the T-Birds. In a fantasy of song and dance, the car is transformed into a spectacular hot rod.

Danny seeks advice from the coach. Later, he gets together with Sandy.

Sandy and Danny meet at the jukebox in the Frosty Palace malt shop. Danny tries to apologize for his earlier behavior by explaining that he has to keep up his image. When he makes fun of the football player she is with, Sandy challenges Danny's athletic ability. He immediately goes to the coach to find a sport in which he can excel.

Later, Sandy and Danny go to the Frosty Palace together. Danny wants to avoid their friends, but the T-Birds and the Pink Ladies come up to their table. After a while, everyone leaves except Frenchy. She quit Rydell High to attend beauty school, but she is not doing well there. Her guardian angel appears singing "Beauty School Dropout." He sings, "Turn in your teasing comb and go back to high school."

Frenchy is back at Rydell with her friends for the televised National Bandstand dance contest. To the tune "Born to Hand Jive," couples dance their hearts out until they are eliminated from competition. Sandy and Danny are one of the few remaining couples when a guy comes up behind Sandy and pulls her off the floor and ChaCha, Danny's old girlfriend, moves in as his dancing partner. Danny and Cha-Cha win the contest and are featured in a spotlight dance. Sandy leaves the gym crying.

Later, at the drive-in movies, Sandy accepts Danny's apology about what happened at the dance. She also accepts his class ring. But when he tries to kiss her, she runs off, throwing his ring back at him. He sings "Stranded at the drive-in/What will they say Monday at school?"

At school on Monday, everyone is talking about Rizzo's possible pregnancy. Rizzo's Pink Lady pal told everyone her secret. Kenickie offers to help, but Rizzo tells him, "It was somebody else's mistake."

The T-Birds get ready to take Kenickie's hot rod to

Thunder Road to race against the rival gang, the Scorpions. Rizzo, who is now a social outcast, watches from afar as Kenickie drives off to the race. She sings, "There Are Worse Things I Could Do": "I could hurt someone like me/out of spite and jealousy/I don't steal and I don't lie/but I can feel and I can cry/a fact I bet you never knew."

At Thunder Road, Kenickie accidentally hits his head and is too dazed to drive in the race. He asks Danny to drive. "Rules are, there ain't no rules," announces the Scorpions' leader. A blade attached to the Scorpion's hubcap slices into Danny's car and the Scorpion tries to run him off the road. But Danny tears ahead of the Scorpion and cuts him off by jumping over some barrels. Danny wins the race.

Sandy has been watching the race alone. Seeing the T-Birds and the Pink Ladies celebrating Danny's victory, she realizes she wants to be part of the group. She sings "Good-bye to Sandra Dee," and asks Frenchy to help her.

On the last day of school, students burst outdoors to the Rydell High School carnival. On the Ferris wheel, Rizzo shouts to Kenickie, "I'm not pregnant!" He cheers, then proposes marriage. They kiss.

Danny surprises his friends by showing up in a letter sweater; he earned a letter in track. Sandy shocks everyone by appearing in red high heels, skin-tight black leather pants, a sexy shirt, and teased hair. "I've got chills," Danny sings to her, "they're multiplying/and I'm losing control/because the power you're supplying/it's electrifying." Together they sing "You're the One That I Want."

The whole school joins in the final dance, singing, "We'll always be like one, together." Sandy and Danny drive off in a red convertible that lifts them into the clouds.

Danny can't believe the change in Sandy.

Olivia Newton-John and John Travolta were too old to play high school students realistically—but realism isn't the point of *Grease* anyway.

A NEW OLD FAVORITE OF MINE

Some people criticized *Grease* for making the 1950s appear to be trouble-free. But *Grease* isn't a documentary. It is about how audiences would like to remember those years, which many people remembered as a happy time in their youth. Many stars of the 1950s had small roles in the film. For example, Eve Arden, who starred in a popular TV series about a school teacher, "Our Miss Brooks," played the principal at Rydell High. The movie's high school was named for the 1950s pop star Bobby Rydell.

Even though Sandy and Danny were supposed to be high school seniors in *Grease*, Olivia Newton-John was 29 and John Travolta was 24 when the film was made, and no serious attempt was made to pretend they were 17. The cartoon credits make it clear that the movie is about fun and fantasy, not reality. In 1978 moviegoers were happy to escape into an idealized version of the past.

DIRTY DANCING

color
pro Lina Gottlieb
dir Emile Ardolino
sc Eleanor Bergstein
music direction Danny Goldberg and Michael Lloyd
music John Morris
st Jennifer Grey (Frances "Baby" Houseman), Patrick
  Swayze (Johnny Castle), Jerry Orbach (Jake
  Houseman), Cynthia Rhodes (Penny Johnson)

Dancing plays a much bigger part than singing in *Dirty Dancing,* which is set in the 1960s. Several critics have pointed out that the movie isn't very realistic, because dancing was not, in fact, nearly as important in the early 1960s as the music itself, especially rock and roll music. If anyone could have made dancing important at the time, however, it would have been the creative team assembled for *Dirty Dancing.* Director Emile Ardolino had won an Academy Award for his earlier documentary feature film, *He Makes Me Feel Like Dancin'.* Patrick Swayze was a principal dancer for the Elliot Feld Ballet before turning to film. And choreographer Kenny Ortega had worked with Madonna on her award-winning music video, "Material Girl."

"I Had the Time of My Life"

A family sedan drives through the Catskill Mountains in upstate New York. Over the strains of "Big Girls Don't Cry," a young woman says, "That was the summer of 1963, when everyone called me 'Baby' and it didn't occur to me to mind. That was before John F. Kennedy was shot, before the Beatles came, when I couldn't wait to join the Peace Corps and thought I'd never find a guy as great as my dad. That was the summer we went to Kellerman's."

At Kellerman's resort, Jake Houseman, his wife Marjorie, and their two daughters are greeted by Max Kellerman, who tells his staff that Dr. Houseman is his special guest. Max immediately sends them off to dancing lessons, where guests of all ages line up to learn a dance called the merengue. Baby's partner is an elderly woman.

That evening before dinner, Baby leaves the family cabin to look around the main lodge. She overhears Max talking to the staff. "There are two kinds of help here," he says. The waiters were hired from Harvard and Yale to show the guests' daughters a good time—even the "ugly" ones. The entertainment staff, led by Johnny Castle, has its own rules. The entertainers may dance with the daughters, "but that's it—no conversation."

At dinner Max introduces the Housemans to their waiter, Robby Gould, a student from Yale Medical School. "Our Baby is going to change the world," Dr. Houseman tells Max. "She's starting Mount Holyoke in the fall." Max calls over his grandson Neil, who attends the Cornell School of Hotel Management.

After dinner Neil and Baby dance together rather stiffly. When the mambo begins, Johnny and another dance instructor, Penny, move to the center of the dance floor. Their performance is extraordinary. Baby is awestruck. Max

Johnny "dirty dances" with Baby at the staff party.

Kellerman does not approve and signals for them to stop.

Later that evening, Baby wanders toward the staff quarters, which are off-limits to guests. She runs into the bellhop. "No guests allowed," he says. Sensing that she is disappointed, he lets her come to a party, as long as she keeps it a secret.

The party is a scene of smoky blue light and sweaty bodies. To the tune of "Work It Out," the staff is doing a new kind of dancing—"dirty dancing." The dancers move together in a sexy way. Baby is fascinated but a bit fearful. Then Johnny and Penny dance. Everyone applauds their skill, including Baby. The bellhop tells her that his cousin Johnny is not romantically involved with Penny. Johnny gives Baby a quick dance lesson to the tune of "Love Man." After the song, Johnny dances off into the crowd.

The next evening Baby looks on as Johnny dances with Vivian Pressman, a middle-aged guest. Neil abruptly interrupts Johnny to ask why Penny isn't on the dance floor. Then Neil takes Baby for a walk and tells her that the two hotels his family owns make him a very desirable "catch" as a husband. Later, in the hotel kitchen with Neil, Baby sees Penny crouched on the floor crying. Johnny carries Penny out of the kitchen. "It's okay, Johnny's here," he comforts her. "I'm never going to let anything happen to you."

Baby follows them back to Penny's room, where she learns that Robby the waiter got Penny pregnant. Baby confronts Robby to ask for money to help Penny, but he refuses. "Some people count, some people don't," he says. Baby then asks her father for the $250 Penny needs to pay for an abortion. "You always said try to help people in trouble," Baby tells her father, "but I can't tell you exactly what the money is for." He agrees to give it to her.

That night Baby returns to the staff party. This time she walks right up to Penny, taps her on the shoulder, and gives her the money. Penny is shocked that a stranger is so generous. She hesitates because her doctor's appointment is on the same night as a mambo act at the Sheldrake Hotel. If Penny and Johnny don't perform at the Sheldrake, they will lose their jobs for the following summer. They make fun of Baby when she insists that a solution can be found. As a joke, Johnny suggests that Baby fill in for Penny. Penny thinks it's possible. The more Johnny insists that Baby can't do it, the more determined Baby becomes to prove him wrong.

They begin to practice. Baby starts off in jeans and sneakers then progresses to leotards and high heels. As their practice sessions intensify so do Baby's feelings for Johnny. He remains professional and drills her relentlessly. The day

Guided by Penny and Johnny, Baby begins practicing.

before the performance, they go off to a lake in the woods to practice. There Johnny explains how he became a professional dancer to avoid his dead-end future.

The next afternoon, while Penny is altering her dress to fit Baby, Penny says she thought Robby loved her. And she is very grateful to Baby for helping her out. Baby consoles the frightened Penny.

At the Sheldrake Hotel, "Johnny Castle and Partner" give an adequate performance of the mambo. Wearing makeup with her hair upswept, Baby is nervous and stiff. She misses

70

The more they dance together, the closer Johnny and Baby become. They are falling in love.

a few steps but recovers gracefully. The audience applauds, impressed by her dancing skill.

In the car on the way back to Kellerman's, Baby expresses some disappointment about her performance. Johnny insists that she did a really good job. His feelings toward her are beginning to change. The radio plays, "I know I can't express/this feeling of tenderness/There's so much I want to say/but the words just won't come my way/Some kind of wonderful."

The mood changes abruptly when Johnny's cousin runs up to the car. "I heard her screaming," he tells them, "I tried to call the ambulance but Penny said the hospital would call the police." When Baby sees that Penny is in pain from the abortion, she immediately gets her father out of bed and brings him to the staff quarters. Dr. Houseman treats Penny.

Upon leaving, Dr. Houseman looks at Johnny in disgust and refuses to speak with him. He thinks Johnny got Penny pregnant. Dr. Houseman turns to Baby. "You're not the person I thought you were," he tells her. "I don't know who you are. You're to have nothing to do with those people, any of them, ever again."

Baby goes to Johnny's room. "I'm sorry about the way my father treated you," she says. Johnny isn't at all offended. On the contrary, Johnny appreciates the doctor's help and admires his skill. Baby interrupts, "I mean the way he was with you." "The reason people treat me like I'm nothing is because I am nothing." Johnny shouts.

He explains how his life alternates between poverty and glamour. "It doesn't have to be that way," she tries to convince him. "I've never known anyone like you," says Johnny. "You're not scared of anything." She replies, "Mostly I'm scared of walking out of this room and never feeling the rest of my whole life the way I feel when I'm with you." She stands to face him. "Dance with me," she says quietly. As they dance, she begins to kiss him. They embrace.

The next morning, Baby visits Penny, who is feeling much better. Johnny comes in. When Baby leaves, Penny confronts Johnny about his involvement with Baby. She doesn't want him to get hurt like she did. Baby is waiting for Johnny when he comes out of Penny's room. He coldly tells her he has to give a dancing lesson, then walks away. She looks after him anxiously, and he turns back and smiles. Later that afternoon they are together in his room. "What's your real name?" Johnny asks. She tells him it's Frances. "That's a real grown-up name," he says approvingly.

Neil barges into the dance studio and almost catches Baby and Johnny together. Neil threatens to hire someone else next season if Johnny doesn't do what Neil wants. Baby

72

is appalled by Neil's rude behavior and tells Johnny to stand up to him. "Fight harder," she encourages Johnny. Just then her father walks by with Lisa and Robby. Johnny and Baby hide in the bushes. "Fight harder," repeats Johnny sarcastically, "I don't see you telling your Daddy I'm your guy." He stalks off.

Baby runs to Penny's cabin and apologizes to Johnny. Robby walks by and makes a crack to Baby about slumming. Johnny starts beating him up, then stops—Robby isn't worth it.

That night in his room, Johnny tells Baby about a dream he had. He dreamed that her father put his arm around him just like he had put his arm around Robby. The next morning, Baby leaves Johnny's room after one last kiss on the steps. Vivian Pressman, on her way out of Robby's room, sees them together.

Max Kellerman and Neil join the Houseman family for breakfast. Max tells them that one of his employees, Johnny Castle, is a thief. Moe Pressman's wallet is missing and Vivian saw Johnny nearby last night. Immediately Baby protests. "Mr. Kellerman, I know Johnny didn't take the wallet. He was in his room all night. The reason I know is that I was with him." Her family is outraged.

Dr. Houseman sits on the veranda alone staring out at the lake. Baby comes to talk to him. "I'm sorry I lied to you Daddy, but you lied to me too." She feels that his idea of fairness is restricted to people like himself.

Johnny finds Baby asleep in the prop room. He tells her that the real criminals were found. "I knew it would be all right," she says excitedly. "I'm out, Baby," he tells her. "They fired you anyway because of me," she screams, "I did it for nothing." "No, no," he tells her. "Nobody's done anything like that for me before."

Johnny goes to see Dr. Houseman. He wants the doctor to know that his daughter really is admirable and caring. But seeing Johnny makes the doctor angry. "I see someone in front of me who got his partner in trouble, sent her to a butcher, then moved on to an innocent young girl like my daughter," he snarls. "Yeah," Johnny replies, "I guess that's what you would see."

In the parking lot, Johnny and Baby say good-bye. "I'll never be sorry," he tells her. "Neither will I," says Baby. Gently he kisses her and drives off.

At the end of the final show at the resort, Neil leads a sing-along. Dr. Houseman stops Robby to give him a tip. "Thanks for the help with the Penny situation," Robby says.

By dancing together, Baby and Johnny overcome their differences in background.

The doctor grabs back the envelope. Johnny enters the back of the auditorium and looks around for Baby. He walks up to her table, takes her by the hand, and leads her to the stage. He goes to the microphone and apologizes for interrupting the song. "I always dance the last dance of the season," he tells the audience. "I'm going to do my kind of dancing with a great partner who is not only a terrific dancer but somebody who's taught me to stand up for other people no matter what it costs them, somebody who's taught me about the kind of person I want to be—Miss Frances Houseman."

The other guests leave the stage while Baby stands in the center spotlight. Johnny moves toward her as the music plays "(I Had) the Time of My Life." They dance together gracefully. The audience oohs and ahs. Soon everyone begins dancing. Dr. Houseman apologizes to Johnny. "I know you weren't the one who got Penny into trouble." Then he turns to Baby. "You looked wonderful out there." Johnny and Baby say the words of the song to one another, "I had the time of my life/no I never felt this way before/I swear, it's the truth/and I owe it all to you." Family, guests, and staff swirl in dance around them.

ACCEPTING SOCIAL DIFFERENCES

It is encouraging that *Dirty Dancing* is one of the musicals that led us into the 1990s. This somewhat nostalgic film about the shift from one social era to another is an interesting twist on the folk musical. As in *Meet Me in St. Louis* and *West Side Story,* the film's central value is expressed in the moral character of the woman. In *Dirty Dancing,* Baby's romantic appeal stems from her moral values. Johnny Castle loves Baby Houseman not only because she is attractive, but also because of her moral principles. She is willing to fight for what she believes in, and she doesn't judge people based on where they come from or how much money they have.

In *Meet Me in St. Louis,* Esther and John Truett come from the same social class. Their marriage ensures that life will continue as it has for them. *West Side Story's* Maria and Tony seem to be different, but they're really not. If only the others would recognize how much they are alike, they could live happily ever after. But Baby and Johnny are acutely aware of their differences. She's from a wealthy, educated family, while he comes from a working-class background. They know that their love for each other can only thrive in a social climate that accepts all kinds of people.

For Further Reading

Altman, Rick. *The American Film Musical*. Bloomington: Indiana University Press, 1987.

Croce, Arlene. *The Fred Astaire and Ginger Rogers Book*. New York: Galahad Books, 1972.

Feuer, Jane. *The Hollywood Musical*. Bloomington: Indiana University Press, 1982.

Fordin, Hugh. *The World of Entertainment: Hollywood's Greatest Musicals*. New York: Doubleday & Co., 1975.

Minnelli, Vincente. *I Remember It Well*. New York: Doubleday & Co., 1974.

Mordden, Ethan. *The Hollywood Musical*. New York: St. Martin's Press, 1981.

Stern, Lee E. *The Movie Musical*. New York: Pyramid Books, 1974.

Taylor, John Russell, and Arthur Jackson. *The Hollywood Musical*. New York: McGraw-Hill, 1971.

More Movie Musicals

A selection of movie musicals that are available on home video:

An American in Paris (1951) *dir* Vincente Minnelli; *st* Gene Kelly, Oscar Levant, Leslie Caron
An American art student studies under the watchful eye of his rich patron until he falls in love with a young woman. Musical highlights include Gershwin's "I've Got Rhythm," "Embraceable You" and "S'Wonderful."

Fame (1980) *dir* Alan Parker; *st* Irene Cara, Lee Curreri
Students at Manhattan's High School for the Performing Arts prepare for life after graduation. Later became a TV series.

Flashdance (1983) *dir* Adrian Lyne; *st* Jennifer Beals, Michael Nouri
A young woman works as a welder in a factory but dreams of becoming a ballerina.

42nd Street (1933) *dir* Lloyd Bacon; *st* Ginger Rogers, Ruby Keeler, Dick Powell
This classic backstage musical, choreographed by Busby Berkeley, chronicles the creation of a Broadway musical and the careers of its stars.

Funny Girl (1968) *dir* William Wyler; *st* Barbra Streisand, Omar Sharif
Streisand stars as Fanny Brice, a vaudeville singer.

Gold Diggers of 1933 (1933) *dir* Mervyn LeRoy; *st* Joan Blondell, Ruby Keeler, Dick Powell, Warren William
The story of a Broadway staging of a musical about the Depression, with choreography by Busby Berkeley.

Mary Poppins (1964) *dir* Robert Stevenson; *st* Julie Andrews, Dick Van Dyke
A magical nanny makes life fun for everyone in turn-of-the-century London.

Saturday Night Fever (1978) *dir* John Badham; *st* John Travolta, Karen Lynn Gorney
A young man with a dead-end job in Brooklyn lives for the weekend, when he is the king of the disco dance floor. The musical score is performed by the BeeGees.

The Sound of Music (1965) *dir* Robert Wise; *st* Julie Andrews, Christopher Plummer
In Austria, a young nun becomes a governess for a widow's children. She and the widow fall in love, and the whole family escapes the Nazi rise to power. Many beloved songs, including "My Favorite Things."

The Wiz (1978) *dir* Sidney Lumet; *st* Michael Jackson, Diana Ross, Richard Pryor
A black casting of *The Wizard of Oz,* based on a hit Broadway musical.

The Wizard of Oz (1939) *dir* Victor Fleming; *st* Judy Garland, Ray Bolger, Bert Lahr
"There's no place like home." And there's no place like Oz, with its wicked and good witches, red shoes, yellow brick road, and cast of lovable characters. Probably the most popular musical of all time.

Index